SCHOLASTIC

Macht

Instant Math Practice
GRAPHS & CHARTS

50 Engaging Reproducibles That Help Kids Read and Interpret Graphs and Charts

Denise Kiernan

D1318717

New York • Toronto • London • Auckland • Sydney

Mexico City • New Delhi • Hong Kong • Buenos Aires

Teaching *Resources*

Edited by Mela Ottaiano
Cover design by Jason Robinson
Interior design by Melinda Belter
Interior illustrations by Teresa Anderko
ISBN: 978-0-439-62923-2

3 4 5 6 7 8 9 10   40   17 16 15 14 13 12 11

Table of Contents

Welcome!

Charts and graphs are visual tools (pictures) that people have developed to convey information more readily. With the dozens of diverse practice pages in *Instant Math Practice: Graphs & Charts*, students will have engaging opportunities to explore, practice, and apply essential math skills and concepts. What's more, students gain experience with math that focuses on graphical and statistical learning, skills that are often overlooked or pushed aside in the earlier grades.

Starting students out early in their elementary careers with graphs and charts gives them a valuable advantage, one that will serve them well and give them a leg up in the years to come. It encourages students to develop awareness of and apply math concepts beyond the classroom. Students learn to keep their eye out for different tables, charts, and graphs that appear in their everyday life, whether they are on food labels or in the sports section of the newspaper.

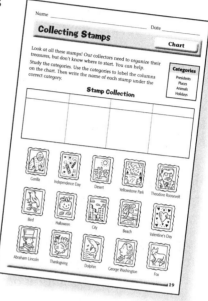

What's Inside?

By pairing the pages of this book with your math instruction, students will gain confidence-building practice with charts and graphs. To help you with lesson planning, turn to the table of contents, where you'll find the titles of the reproducible practice pages along with the skill areas they support.

With your instructional needs in mind, the activities . . .

- **will help you meet math standards.** Each page offers appropriate math challenges to second- and third-grade students at every skill level. The National Council of Teachers of Mathematics (NCTM) has proposed what teachers should provide for their students to become proficient in mathematics. To learn how the practice pages in this book support these standards, visit the Web site: http://standards.nctm.org. For more information about NCTM and to learn more about the topics and benchmarks within each math standard, read *Principles and Standards for School Mathematics* from the National Council for Teachers of Mathematics, 2000. To find out how these activities connect to the Common Core State Standards, visit http://www.corestandards.org.

- **are cross-curricular and flexible in their usage.** There's a practice page to complement most every student's interest and planned math lesson. You can use the pages throughout the school year, weaving them into your lessons as needed since they're on the topics you teach, including money math, geography, reading, time lines, current events, science, and sports.

- **all come with answers.** The complete Answer Key begins on page 57.

Quick Reference

The following descriptions highlight the general purpose of the graphs included in this book.

Circle Graph (or Pie Chart)

A circle graph shows parts of a whole.

Example: The total circle represents the number of Super Bowl victories, divided into victories for AFC teams and victories for NFC teams.

Pictograph

A pictograph uses pictures. Each picture represents a certain number of people or things.

Example: The total rainfall in inches for several different cities, with one umbrella equivalent to 2 inches of rainfall. (Always refer to the Key. It shows the amount a picture represents.)

Bar Graph

A bar graph uses bars to show and compare total numbers of things.

Example: The total number of Olympic gold medals won, with one bar representing the medal total of each country.

Double Bar Graph

A double bar graph uses bars to show total numbers of things, but divides each total number into two groups.

Example: The total number of Olympic gold medals won by country, with each country represented by two bars, one bar for men's events, the other bar for women's.

Line Graph

A line graph shows changes over time.

Example: How sports participation in school has changed from 1960 to 2010.

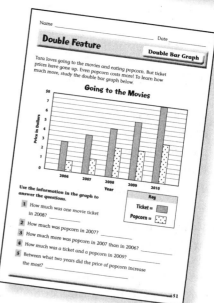

Name _____ Date _____

Measuring Gorillas

Could you measure a gorilla? Just how tall might he or she be?
If you're wild about animals of all sizes, study the chart below.

Animal Heights

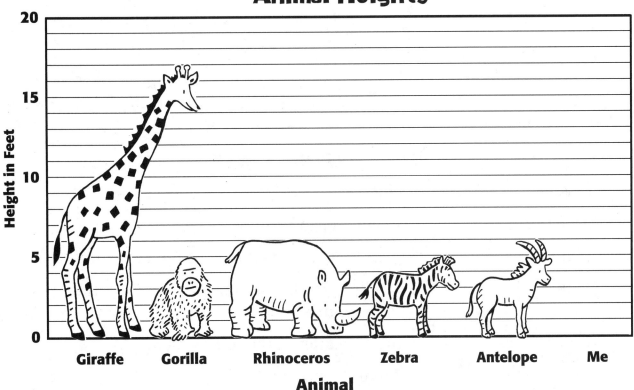

Use the information on the graph to answer the questions.

1 How tall is the giraffe? _____

2 How tall is the rhinoceros? _____

3 How much taller is the giraffe than the gorilla? _____

4 How much shorter is the zebra than the rhinoceros?

_____

5 How tall are you? _____ Draw a picture of yourself on

the chart and mark your height.

The Final Frontier

Chart

On clear nights, you can often see our moon and many stars. You might even see a planet! To learn more about our solar system, study the chart below.

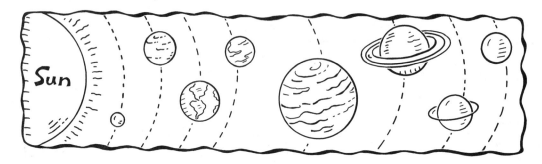

Tips

• The planet closest to the Sun is number "1."

• Questions 1–4 contain hints.

Solar System Facts

Planet	Order	Hint
Mercury	_____	a neighbor to Venus
Uranus	_____	first planet discovered by using a telescope
Venus	_____	not the very closest to the sun, but still the hottest planet
Jupiter	_____	largest planet in the solar system
Earth	**3**	Home sweet home!
Saturn	_____	has several rings around it
Mars	_____	often called the "red planet"
Neptune	_____	sea god in Roman myths

Read the hints above and in the questions. Then order the planets from 1 to 8. (Write the number in the blank next to each name.) Use the information in the chart to answer the questions.

1 Rings around the planet! Which planet is 6th from the Sun? _____

2 Oceans away from Earth, which planet is 8th from the Sun? _____

3 Which cherry-colored planet is 4th from the Sun? _____

4 Which giant planet is 5th from the Sun? _____

Trading Card Statistics

Carly collects all kinds of trading cards. Here are six cards from some of her favorite teams. Study the charts on each of the cards below.

Carly's Cards

Rock Tackler
FOOTBALL

Date of Birth:
January 10, 1985

Hometown:
Lexington, MO

Team:
Marvelous Mud Pies

Points scored last year:
27

Ima Slider
BASEBALL

Date of Birth:
February 11, 1990

Hometown:
Crownsville, MD

Team:
Roarin' Rories

Susie S. Lamdunk
BASKETBALL

Date of Birth:
August 24, 1989

Hometown:
Columbia, SC

Team:
Half-pint Hoopsters

Kimmy Kixx
SOCCER

Date of Birth:
July 31, 1996

Hometown:
New York, NY

Team:
Village Vortex

Slice Parr
GOLF

Date of Birth:
November 5, 1997

Hometown:
Providence, RI

Team:
P-town Putters

Joey Sticks
HOCKEY

Date of Birth:
July 30, 1994

Hometown:
Closter, NJ

Team:
Screaming Scootchies

Use the information in the charts to answer the questions.

1 What sport does Slice play? _____

2 How old is Kimmy? _____

3 Who is from Closter, NJ? _____

4 Which team has Rock as a member? _____

5 How much older is Joey than Kimmy? _____

Name _____ Date _____

Summer Camp Survey

Oh no! Where's my toothbrush? This summer, the camp counselors conducted a survey to find out which items children forget to bring to camp. Study the bar graph below. Have you ever forgotten to bring any of these items with you when you needed them?

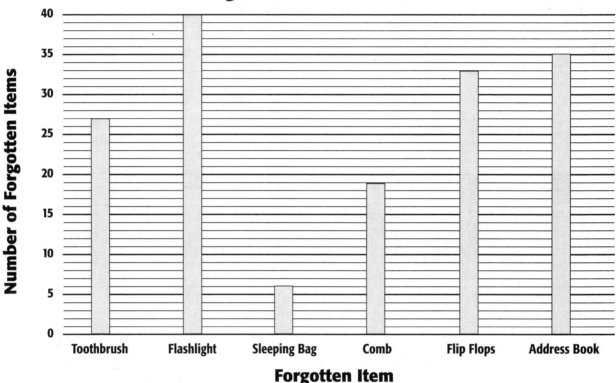

Things Kids Left at Home

Use the information in the bar graph to answer the questions.

1 Which item did the greatest number of kids forget to bring? _____

2 Which item did the fewest number of kids forget to bring? _____

3 How many kids might have messy hair at summer camp? _____

4 How many kids won't be able to write postcards to their friends and family? _____

5 Which two items did almost the same number of kids forget?

_____

Name _____ Date _____

Bake Sale Bonanza

Last Friday, Elmwood Elementary held a bake sale. Which baked goods were the most popular?

Elmwood Elementary Bake Sale

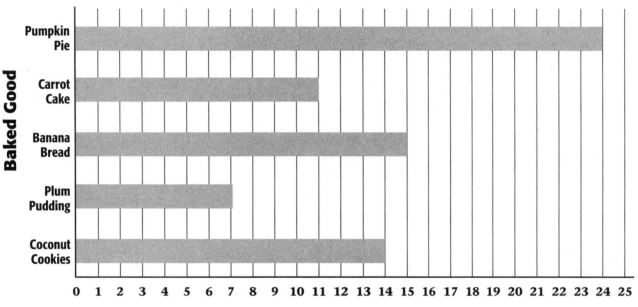

Number of Baked Goods Sold

Use the information in the bar graph to answer the questions.

1 Which baked item sold the most? _____

How many was that? _____

2 Which baked item was the least popular? _____

How many were sold? _____

3 How many more pumpkin pies sold than coconut cookies? _____

4 In all, how many items sold at the bake sale? _____

5 Which item in the graph would you buy? _____

Add this information to the graph.

Name _____ Date _____

First-Choice Music

Circle Graph

Miss Treble's music class listens to all kinds of music. But what kind of music do her students like best? To find out, each student in Miss Treble's class voted. Study the results in the circle graph below.

Favorite Kind of Music

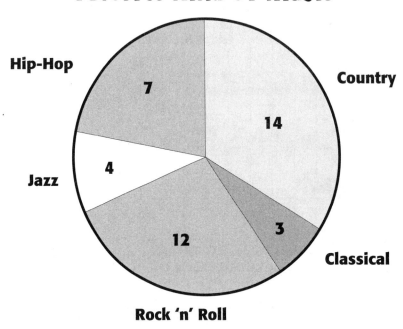

Hip-Hop 7

Country 14

Jazz 4

Classical 3

Rock 'n' Roll 12

Use the information in the circle graph to answer the questions.

1 How many students chose country music as their favorite? _____

2 How many students chose rock 'n' roll as their favorite? _____

3 How many more students chose hip-hop than classical
as their favorite? _____

4 How many students all together chose classical and jazz
as their favorites? _____

5 All together, how many students are in Miss Treble's
music class? _____

After School Schedule

Rashawn has things to do every day after school. To keep track of where to be and what time he has to be there, Rashawn made a schedule. Study the chart below.

Rashawn's Schedule

	Monday	Tuesday	Wednesday	Thursday	Friday
3:30	math tutor		math tutor	math tutor	
4:30		basketball practice		basketball practice	
5:30			piano lesson		
6:30	dinner at Grandma's	dinner at home	dinner at Grandma's	dinner at home	pizza night

Use the information in the chart to answer the questions.

1 Where is Rashawn at 4:30 on Thursdays? _____

2 When does he have his piano lesson?

Day _____ Time _____

3 What is Rashawn doing at 6:30 on Friday? _____

4 Which days does he eat dinner with his Grandma?

_____

5 When can Rashawn go to the park on Wednesday afternoon?

_____

Name _____ Date _____

Nutritious and Delicious

Mrs. Walker's third grade class loves to eat! What are their favorite snacks? Study the circle graph below.

Favorite Snacks

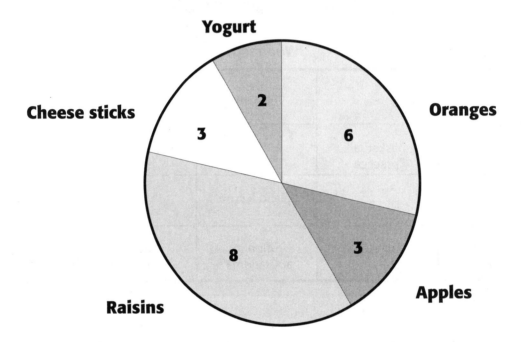

Use the information in the circle graph to answer the questions.

1 How many students chose oranges as their favorite snack? _____

2 Which food was chosen as a favorite by the greatest number of students?
_____ How many students chose it? _____

3 All together, how many students chose oranges and apples? _____

4 Which foods had the same number of students choose them?

_____

5 How many students are there all together in Mrs. Walker's class? _____

Name _____ Date _____

Save or Spend?

Many of the children in Mr. Chavez's neighborhood earn money each week by doing chores for their neighbors. But what do the children do with their money? To learn what Mr. Chavez found out, study the circle graph below.

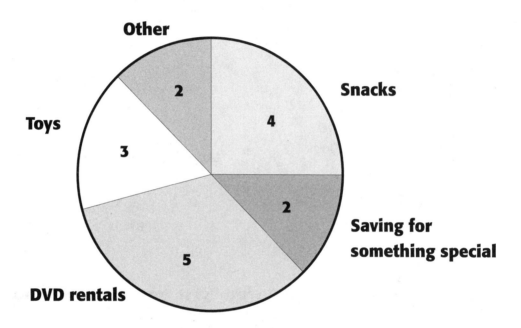

Money Spent

Use the information in the circle graph to answer the questions.

1 How many children spend most of their money on toys? _____

2 How many save most of their money? _____

3 How many more students spend their money on DVD rentals than savings? _____

4 How many students said they spend their money on something other than what is listed? _____

5 All together, how many children in Mr. Chavez's neighborhood do extra chores to earn money? _____

15

Name _____ Date _____

Fins, Feathers, or Fur?

Mr. Monroe's class voted on their favorite animals. To find out which animals got the most votes, study the circle graphs below.

What's Your Favorite Animal?

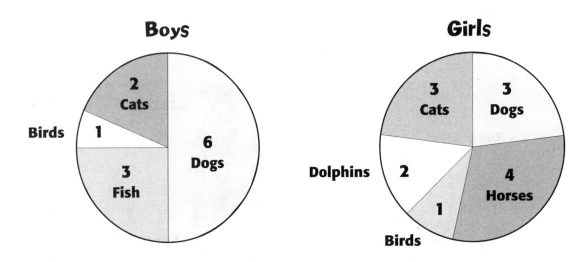

Use the information in the circle graphs to answer the questions.

1 How many girls said horses were their favorite? _____

2 How many boys said birds were their favorite? _____

3 How many more boys than girls prefer dogs? _____

4 How many more girls than boys are there in Mr. Monroe's class? _____

5 Which is greater: The number of girls who like horses or the number of boys who like dogs? _____

How much greater? _____

Name _____ Date _____

Time Online

Surf's up on the Web! To find out how much time each day the students in Mr. Boolean's class spend online, study the circle graphs below.

Daily Surf Time

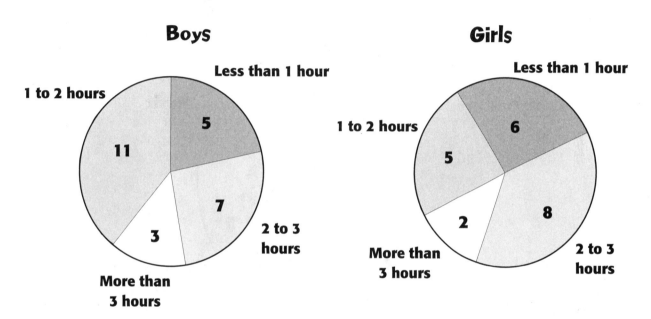

Use the information in the circle graphs to answer the questions.

1 How many boys were surveyed? _____

2 How many girls said they spend more than 3 hours online every day? _____

3 How many girls were surveyed? _____

4 How many girls said they spend less than 1 hour online every day? _____

5 How many boys and girls spend 2 to 3 hours online every day? _____

Name _____   Date _____

Fundraising Picnic

The fundraising picnic was a success! But even though the school made money from ticket and refreshment sales, they had to spend some money, too. Where did the money go? Study the circle graph below.

School Picnic Expenses

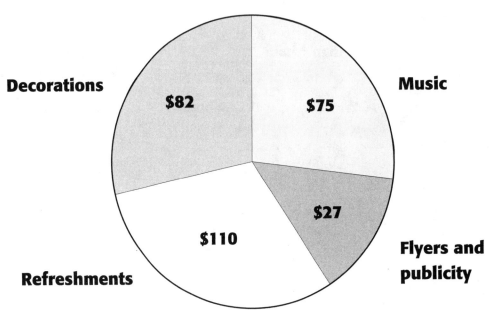

Use the information in the circle graph to answer the questions.

1 How much money was spent on music? _____

2 Which cost more: music or refreshments? _____
How much more? _____

3 How much more money was spent on decorations than on music?

_____

4 In total, how much did the school spend on the picnic? _____

5 After ticket sales, the school had $678. After paying the expenses, how much money did the school have left over to save? _____

Name _____ Date _____

Collecting Stamps

Look at all these stamps! Our collectors need to organize their treasures, but don't know where to start. You can help.

Study the categories. Use the categories to label the columns on the chart. Then write the name of each stamp under the correct category.

Categories

Presidents
Places
Animals
Holidays

Stamp Collection

Gorilla   Independence Day   Desert   Yellowstone Park   Theodore Roosevelt

Bird   Halloween   City   Beach   Valentine's Day

Abraham Lincoln

Thanksgiving

Dolphin

George Washington

Fox

Looking at Labels

Snacks sure do taste good, but what exactly are they made of? Which snacks are nutritious? To find out, you can read about the ingredients. Study the nutrition labels below.

TASTY TORTILLA TREATS

Nutrition Facts

Serving Size	5 chips
Servings per Container	7
Calories	110
Total Fat	2 grams
Saturated Fat	0 grams
Cholesterol	5 milligrams
Sodium	200 milligrams
Carbohydrate	22 grams
Dietary Fiber	2 grams
Protein	3 grams

Nutty Nuts Peanut Butter

Nutrition Facts

Serving Size	2 tablespoons
Servings per Container	15
Calories	180
Total Fat	15 grams
Saturated Fat	2.5 grams
Cholesterol	10 milligrams
Sodium	40 milligrams
Carbohydrate	6 grams
Dietary Fiber	2 grams
Protein	7 grams

Use the information in the nutrition labels to answer the questions.

1 What is the serving size for tortilla chips? _____

2 How many calories are in one serving of Nutty Nuts Peanut Butter? _____

3 Which snack has the most sodium per serving? _____

4 Which snack has the most cholesterol per serving? _____ How much more? _____

5 How much more protein does the peanut butter have per serving than the tortilla chips? _____

Name _____ Date _____

Favorite Sports

There are so many different sports to choose from, but which one is the favorite of the classroom kids we talked to? Study the circle graphs below.

What's Your Favorite Sport?

Boys

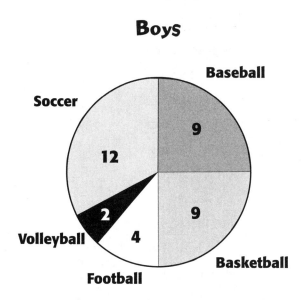

Girls

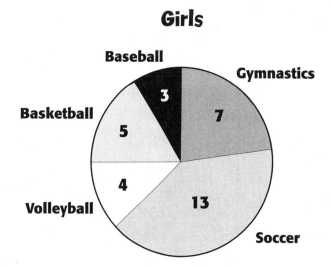

Use the information in the circle graphs to answer the questions.

1 Which is the favorite sport of the boys? _____

2 Which is the favorite sport of the girls? _____

3 How many more girls play soccer than baseball? _____

4 How many more boys play baseball than volleyball? _____

5 All together, how many boys and girls voted on their

favorite sports? _____

Soccer Team Schedule

Sam and Sidney are super soccer supporters. To see every game that the Sunny City Strikers play, Sid and Sidney have to study the soccer schedule below.

Sunny City Strikers Spring Schedule

Friday, March 11	AWAY	Freemont Froghoppers
Saturday, March 19	HOME	Kay Town Kreepers
Sunday, March 27	AWAY	Sandy Bend Sweepers
Saturday, April 2	HOME	Mudville Movers
Saturday, April 9	AWAY	Shore Village Vipers
Sunday, April 17	HOME	Apple Valley Attack
Sunday, April 24	AWAY	Mudville Movers
Friday, April 29	HOME	Shore Village Vipers
Saturday, May 7	AWAY	West Side Wangdoodlers
Friday, May 13	HOME	Sandy Bend Sweepers
Sunday, May 22	AWAY	Kay Town Kreepers
Saturday, May 29	HOME	Freemont Froghoppers
Sunday, June 5	AWAY	Apple Valley Attack
Saturday, June 11	HOME	West Side Wangdoodlers

Use the information in the chart to answer the questions.

1 How many games do the Strikers play on Saturdays? _____

2 Who does the team play on March 27? _____

Are they at home or away? _____

3 When do the Strikers play the Sweepers at home? _____

4 How many more games do the Strikers play on Sundays

than on Fridays? _____

5 How many games total do the Strikers play at home? _____

Marvelous Money Tracker

Mac has decided to keep track of the money he spends and the money he saves. To help Mac keep track of his money, read the note below. Then use the information to fill in the chart. We did one for you.

Mac's Money

Date	Money Added/Money Subtracted	Balance
January 3	First day of my new piggy bank!	$5
January 7	Babysitting, add six dollars	$11

January 7: Mac made $6 babysitting.

January 8: Mac spends $1 on candy.

January 12: Mac earns $4 cleaning the garage.

January 14: Mac spends $2 on trading cards.

January 18: Mac gets $5 allowance.

January 22: Mac earns $3 helping organize the basement.

January 25: Mac spends $4 on comic books.

January 28: Mac earns $5 babysitting.

Use the information in the completed chart to answer the question.

How much money does Mac have in his piggy bank now? _____

Rainy Day Drops

Rain, rain, go away! And don't come back . . . until we've finished our pictograph! It's raining again, and the residents of Dawson have to keep track of how much has fallen. Study the pictograph below.

Rainfall in Dawson

January	💧 💧 💧 💧
February	💧 💧 💧 💧 ⌇
March	💧 💧
April	💧 💧 💧
May	💧 ⌇
June	💧
July	⌇
August	💧 💧
September	💧 💧
October	💧 💧 💧
November	💧 💧 💧
December	💧 💧 💧 ⌇

Key

💧 = 1 inch of rain	
⌇ = ½ inch of rain	

Use the information in the pictograph to answer the questions.

1 How many inches of rain fell in November? _____

2 How many inches of rain fell in June? _____

3 How many fewer inches of rain fell in June than in November?

_____

4 How many more inches of rain fell in February than in July? _____

5 All together, how many inches of rain fell? _____

Name _____ Date _____

Library Book Boom

Some schools in Pixie are collecting books for the city library. How many books have been donated? Study the bar graph below.

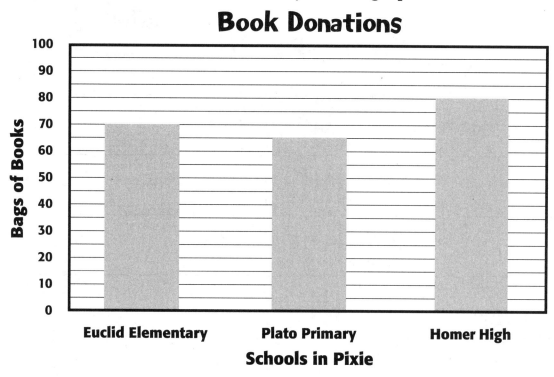

Book Donations

Use the information in the bar graph to answer the questions.

1 How many bags of books has Euclid Elementary collected? _____

2 How many bags of books has Plato Primary collected? _____

3 How many bags of books have all three schools collected together? _____

4 If each bag contains 10 books, how many books have the schools collected all together? _____

5 The library needs 500 more books to meet its goal. How many more bags do the schools need to collect all together? _____

Name _____ Date _____

Hungry for Hot Dogs

Hot dog! That's what the kids in this hot-dog eating contest ate. How many hot dogs did the students scarf down? Study the graph below.

Contest Results

Contestant	Number of Hot Dogs Eaten
Bell E. Ake	ЖЖ ЖЖ I
Ima Stuft	ЖЖ ЖЖ II
I. M. Sikk	ЖЖ I
R. U. Fuller	ЖЖ III

Number of Hot Dogs Eaten

Use the information in the chart to answer the questions.

1   How many hot dogs did Bell E. Ake eat? _____

2   How many more did Ima Stuft eat than R. U. Fuller? _____

3   How many fewer hot dogs did I. M. Sikk eat than Bell E. Ake?

    _____

4   Which is greater: The number of hot dogs that Ima ate or the number

    that I. M. and R. U. ate together? _____

    How much greater? _____

5   All together, how many hot dogs were eaten? _____

Name _____ Date _____

Doggie Walkathon

This year the local pet clubs have formed teams to see who can register the most walkers. To see how the competition is going, study the graph below.

Pet Club Teams

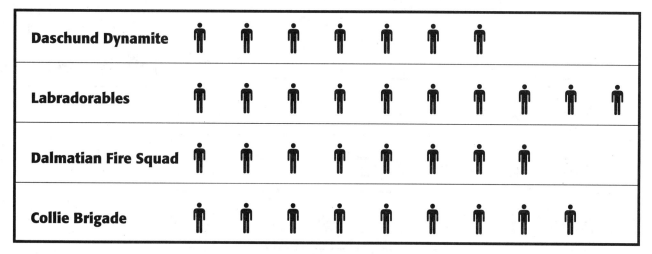

Use the information in the pictograph to answer the questions. Remember to look at the Key.

Key
👤 = 10 people

1 How many walkers did the Daschund Dynamite register? _____

2 How many walkers did the Dalmatian Fire Squad register? _____

3 How many walkers did the Collie Brigade register? _____

4 All together, how many walkers are registered? _____

5 If the goal was to register 400 walkers, how many more walkers are needed to reach the goal? _____

Name _____ Date _____

Picto-Perfect Tree

Every Arbor Day, kids at Green Street School get together to plant trees. Each year they plant more and more trees. How many trees have the kids planted over the past few years? Study the pictograph below.

Arbor Day Tree Planting

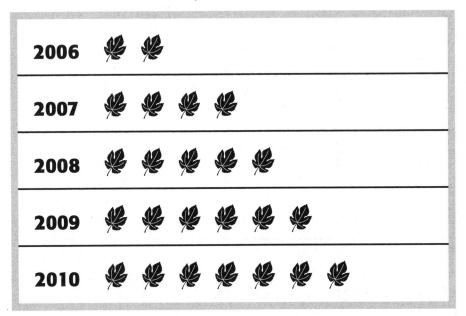

Key

🍁 = 2 trees

Use the information in the pictograph to answer the questions. Remember to look at the Key.

1 How many trees did the kids plant in 2006? _____

2 How many trees did they plant in 2009? _____

3 How many more trees were planted in 2008 than in 2007? _____

4 How many more trees were planted in 2010 than in 2008? _____

5 How many trees in total did the kids at Green Street School plant? _____

Name _____ Date _____

Can You Recycle?

All the grades at Hamilton Elementary School have been collecting cans all year for the recycling center. To find out how many cans they collected, study the pictograph below.

Can Collection

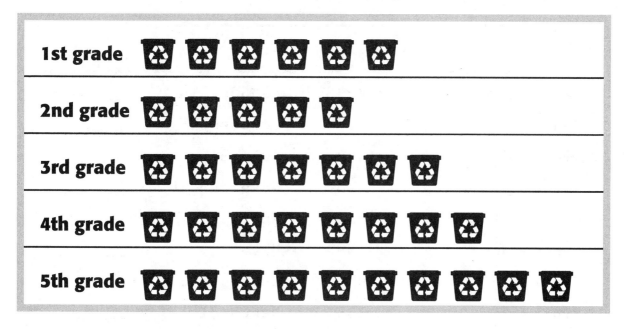

Use the information in the pictograph to answer the questions. Remember to look at the Key.

Key
♲ = 100 cans

1 How many cans did the 1st grade collect?

_____

2 How many more cans did the 5th grade collect than the second grade?

_____

3 How many cans did the 4th grade collect? _____

4 How many more cans did the 3rd grade collect than the 2nd grade?

_____

5 All together, how many cans did all the classes collect? _____

Ranking Gamers

These top ten video gamers love to play Galactic Mathematic
Video Challenge. To see who is winning, study the chart below.
To complete the chart, rank the players from highest to lowest.
Order the players from 1 to 10 in the blanks next to each name.
The player with the highest score is number "1."

Player	Score	Date	Rank
The Count	473	January 10	_____
Numb Thumbs	375	October 13	_____
Vid Kid	540	July 31	_____
Number Gal	360	November 10	_____
Eyes on the Prize	420	April 8	_____
Gary Gamer	599	May 2	_____
Vid Kid	493	November 5	_____
Digitz	358	March 21	_____
Number Gal	525	August 2	_____
The Count	480	July 11	_____

Use the information in the chart to answer the questions.

1 Who had the highest score? _____

2 Who scored 420 points? _____

3 Who played on March 21? _____

4 How many points did Numb Thumbs score? _____

5 Which players were listed more than once?

_____ _____ _____

Happy Birth-Month!

Chart

What month were you born? To find out your birthstone and special flower, study the chart below.

Birth-Month Facts

Month	Birthstone	Flower
January	garnet	carnation
February	amethyst	primrose
March	aquamarine	violet
April	diamond	daisy
May	emerald	hawthorn
June	pearl	rose
July	ruby	water lily
August	peridot	poppy
September	sapphire	morning glory
October	opal	cosmos
November	topaz	chrysanthemum
December	turquoise	poinsettia

Use the chart to answer the questions.

1 Ruby is the birthstone for people born in which month?

_____

2 If your birthday is in November, what is your birthstone?

_____

3 Birthdays in this month share the pearl for a birthstone:

_____

4 If your birthstone is a diamond, what is your flower? _____

5 If your flower is the water lily, what is your birthstone?

_____

Stars and Skies

As the months change, different groups of stars are visible in the dark, night sky. What groups of stars, or constellations, were in the sky when you were born? Study the chart below.

The Zodiac

Sign	Birthdates	Symbol
Capricorn	Dec 22 – Jan 19	mountain goat
Aquarius	Jan 20 – Feb 18	water-bearer
Pisces	Feb 19 – Mar 20	fish
Aries	Mar 21 – Apr 19	ram
Taurus	Apr 20 – May 20	bull
Gemini	May 21 – June 21	twins
Cancer	June 22 – July 22	crab
Leo	July 23 – Aug 22	lion
Virgo	Aug 23 – Sept 22	young woman
Libra	Sept 23 – Oct 22	scales
Scorpio	Oct 23 – Nov 21	scorpion
Sagittarius	Nov 22 – Dec 21	archer

Use the information in the chart to answer the questions.

1 What is the symbol of Leo? _____

2 The archer represents which sign? _____

3 If you were born October 10, what is your sign? _____

4 If your symbol is the bull, between which dates were you born?

_____

Name _____ Date _____

Seashells by the Seashore   Bar Graph

Sally sees seashells by the seashore and collects them each
summer. To learn how many seashells has she collected over the
years, study the bar graph below.

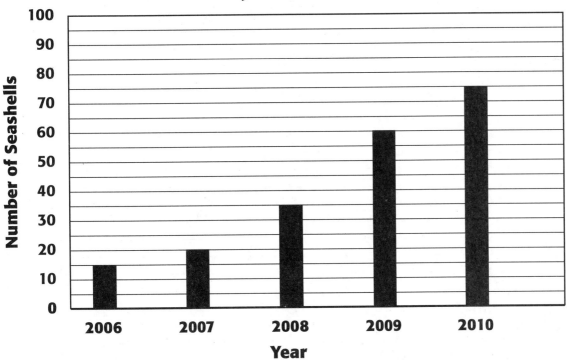

Sally's Seashells

Number of Seashells vs. *Year*

Use the information in the bar graph to answer the questions.

1 How many shells did Sally collect in 2006? _____

2 How many shells did Sally collect in 2009? _____

3 How many more shells did Sally collect in 2010 than
   in 2006? _____

4 In which years did Sally collect an odd number of
   shells? _____

5 All together, how many shells did Sally collect? _____

Name _____ Date _____

Price Highs and Lows

Airfare can be a bear when the prices rise. Study the line graph to see how the average price of a round-trip ticket from Los Angeles to New York City has changed over the years.

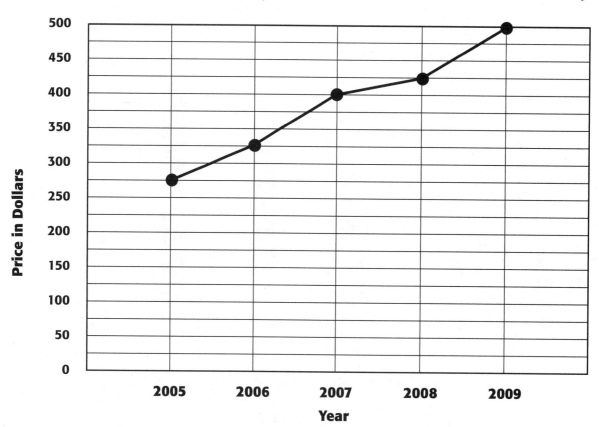

Cloud Nine Airlines, Los Angeles to New York City

Use the information on the line graph to answer the questions.

1 How much did a ticket cost in 2006? _____

2 How much did a ticket cost in 2008? _____

3 How much more did a ticket cost in 2009 than in 2005? _____

4 How much would two tickets cost in 2007? _____

5 How much would two tickets cost in 2009? _____

Name _____ Date _____

Flocks of Friends

There are so many kinds of birds in the United States, who can count them all? Well, Seymore Byrd tries. Every year on July 1st, Seymore counts as many birds as he can. Study the graph to see how many birds Seymore has seen over the years.

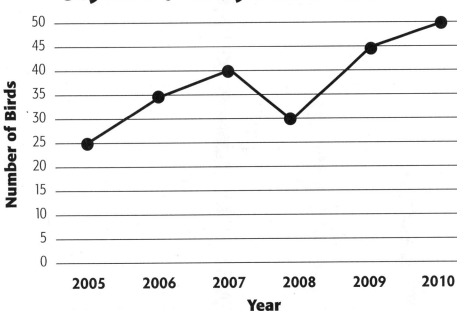

Seymore's Yearly Bird Count

Use the information on the graph to answer the questions.

1 How many different birds did Seymore count in 2005? _____

2 How many more birds did Seymore count in 2007 than in 2008?

_____

3 In which years did Seymore count an even number of birds?

_____

4 In which year did Seymore count the least number of birds? _____

5 Which is the only year that Seymore didn't see more birds than the

year before? _____

Name _____ Date _____

Animals Snooze

Do you like sleeping, napping, and snoozing? Everybody needs rest, even a giant sloth! But how much shut-eye do wild animals need? Study the bar graph below.

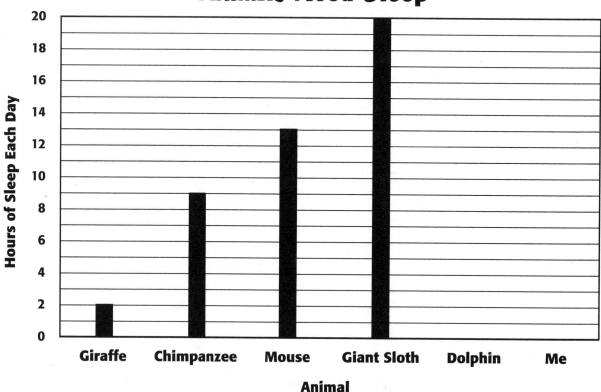

Use the information in the bar graph to answer the questions.

1. How much does a mouse sleep each day? _____

2. How much does a chimpanzee sleep in 2 days? _____ Is that more or less than the number of hours a giant sloth sleeps in one day? _____ How much? _____

3. Which animal sleeps the least? _____

4. Dolphins sleep 6 hours each day. Add this information to the graph.

5. How much do you sleep? _____ Add your answer to the graph.

Great State Trivia

Chart

Do you live in the Show Me State? What's your state flower?
Every state in the United States of America has its own history
and even its own special nickname. To find out information
about some of the states, study the chart below.

State Facts

	North Carolina	Hawaii	New York	Kansas	Washington
Became a State	1789	1959	1788	1861	1889
Capital	Raleigh	Honolulu	Albany	Topeka	Olympia
Flower	Flowering Dogwood	Yellow Hibiscus	Rose	Sunflower	Rhododendron
Bird	Cardinal	Nene	Bluebird	Meadowlark	Gold finch
State Nickname	Tar Heel State	Aloha State	Empire State	Sunflower State	Evergreen State

Use the information in the chart to answer the questions.

1 What is the capital of Kansas? _____

2 What is North Carolina's state flower? _____

3 Which state has the rose as its flower? _____

4 Which state is the youngest? _____

   When did it become a state? _____

5 What is the capital of the state where the gold finch is the state bird?

   _____

6 Which state's nickname is the Sunflower State? _____

Kids Count

It's time to count the kids at Abacus Elementary. To keep track of the students, the teachers use pictographs like the one below.

Number of Students

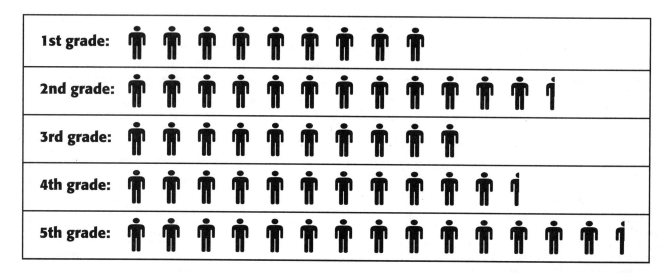

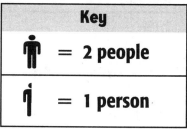

Use the information in the pictograph to answer the questions. Remember to look at the Key.

1 How many students are in the 1st grade? _____

2 How many students are in the 5th grade? _____

3 How many more students are in the 2nd grade than the 1st grade? _____

4 How many more students are in the 5th grade than the 3rd grade? _____

5 How many students are there all together in the school? _____

Name _____ Date _____

Statehood Statistics

Today there are 50 states in the United States of America. There haven't always been so many! Study the line graph below to see how the number of states has increased through the years.

From 0 to 50

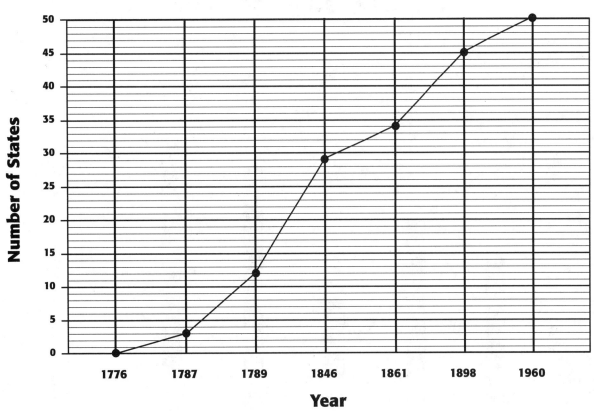

Use the information in the line graph to answer the questions.

1 How many states were there in 1776? _____

2 How many states were there in 1898? _____

3 How many states were there in 1861? _____

4 How many more states were there in 1787 than in 1776? _____

5 How many years did it take to go from 0 to 50 states? _____

Eggs-tra Special

It's the annual Easter Egg Hunt and everyone wants to find the most eggs. We made a bar graph to keep track of how many eggs were found by each grade. Who found the most? Study the bar graph below.

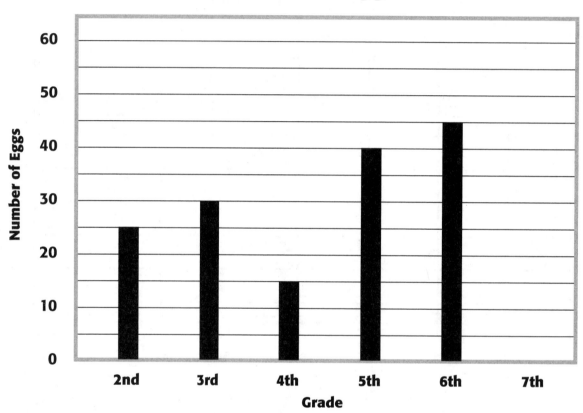

Annual Easter Egg Hunt

Use the information in the bar graph to answer the questions.

1 How many eggs did the 4th grade find? _____

2 How many more eggs did the 5th grade find than the 2nd grade?

_____

3 Which grades found an even number of eggs? _____

4 The 7th grade found 10 more eggs than the 6th grade. How many eggs did the 7th grade find? _____ Mark that number on the bar graph.

Name _____ Date _____

Favorite Colors

What's your favorite color? The students at Shepherd Pie School had to vote for their favorite color. The circle graph below shows how students voted.

Favorite Colors 1

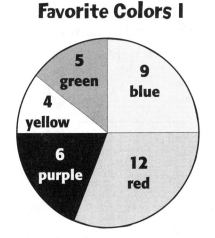

1 How many students chose blue as their favorite color? _____

2 How many more students chose red as their favorite color than yellow? _____

3 How many students all together voted on their favorite color? _____

4 What even numbers do you see in the pie chart? _____

5 Which is greater, the number of students that chose yellow and blue as their favorite colors, or the number of students that chose red as their favorite color? _____

Use the information below to complete this circle graph.

Favorite Colors 2

Blue: 20

Red: 8

Purple: 4

Green: 6

Yellow: 2

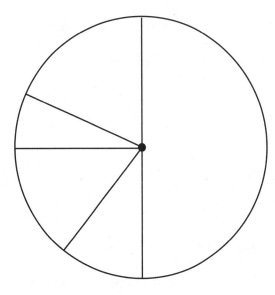

Name _____ Date _____

Piggy Banks and Pennies

Penny has been savings her pennies and her quarters, and dimes and nickels, too! Now it's time to crack open her piggy bank. Study the bar graph below to learn how much money she has saved.

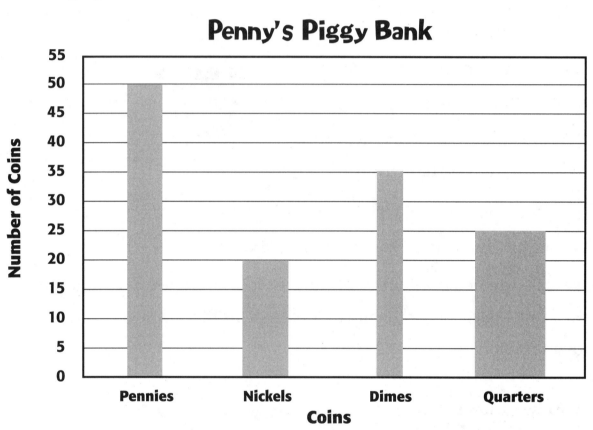

Use the information in the bar graph to answer the questions.

1 How many dimes does Penny have? _____

2 Look at the number of pennies. How many quarters is that worth?

_____

3 Look at the number of quarters. How many dollars and cents is that worth? _____

4 How much are the pennies and nickels worth all together? _____

5 Count all the money. How much is it worth all together? _____

Name _____ Date _____

The Price Is What?   **Line Graph**

Nicholas goes to the corner grocery every week for his parents. He's noticed that the store's prices are rising. How much have the prices of some of his groceries gone up? Study the line graphs below.

Use the information in the three line graphs to answer the questions.

1 How much did a gallon of milk cost in 2008? _____

2 How much did a dozen eggs cost in 2010? _____

3 How much more did a loaf of bread cost in 2008 than 2007? _____

4 In 2007, which item cost the most? _____

5 How much more did all three items cost in 2010 than in 2009? _____

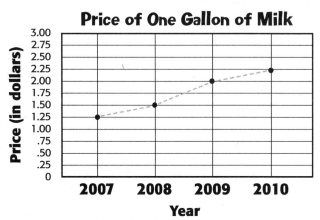

Calling Card Sense

Table

Lisa has friends who live all over the world. Calling them can get expensive, so Lisa is researching which calling card to buy. To help Lisa find the best prices, study the table below.

Calling Card Plans

	Phone Home	**Dial Away**	**Call Again**
Italy	5 cents/minute	4 cents/minute	6 cents/minute
France	3 cents/minute	4 cents/minute	5 cents/minute
Germany	4 cents/minute	5 cents/minute	3 cents/minute
Canada	2 cents/minute	3 cents/minute	3 cents/minute

Use the information in the table to answer the questions.

1 How much does it cost to call France using Dial Away? _____

2 How much does it cost to call Canada using Phone Home? _____

3 How much more does it cost to call Italy using Call Again than

   Dial Away? _____

4 Which is the best card to use to call Germany? _____

5 How much does a ten-minute call to Canada cost using

   Dial Away? _____

6 Using which plan does it cost more to call France than

   to call Germany? _____

Name _____ Date _____

Speedy Animals

Wow! Look at those animals run! Which are the fastest? You might be surprised. Study the bar graph below.

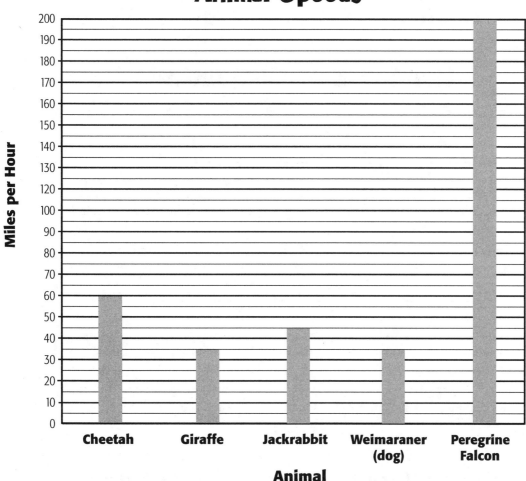

Use the information in the bar graph to answer the questions.

1 How fast can the jackrabbit run? _____

2 How fast can the peregrine falcon fly? _____

3 How much faster is the cheetah than the giraffe? _____

4 How much faster is the falcon than the jackrabbit? _____

5 Which two animals run at about the same speed? _____

Animal Ages

Did you know that some plants can live thousands of years? But, what is the longest amount of time that some animals have been known to live? Study the chart to find out.

Guppy	5 years
Blue Whale	80 years
Mouse	3 years
Crocodile	60 years
Toad	36 years

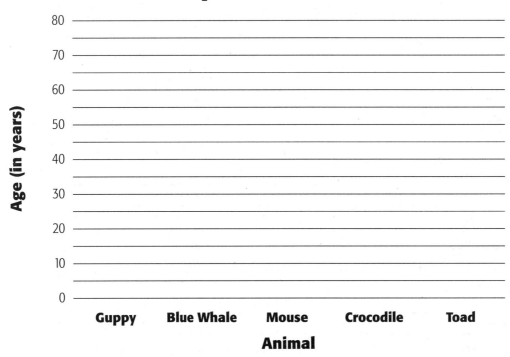

Life Spans of Wild Animals

Age (in years)

80
70
60
50
40
30
20
10
0

Guppy   Blue Whale   Mouse   Crocodile   Toad

Animal

Use the information in the chart to create a bar graph. Remember to draw a bar above each animal's name to show about how many years it might live. Then answer the questions.

1 Which animal lives the longest? _____

2 How many more years might a guppy live than a mouse? _____

3 How many more years might a blue whale live than a toad? _____

4 How many more years might a crocodile live than a mouse? _____

Name _____ Date _____

Navigating the U.S.A.

The United States of America is a big country. But we've found an easy way for you to navigate the map. Study the map of the continental United States below. To use the grid to locate a place, first find the letter and then the number. Find the square where they meet.

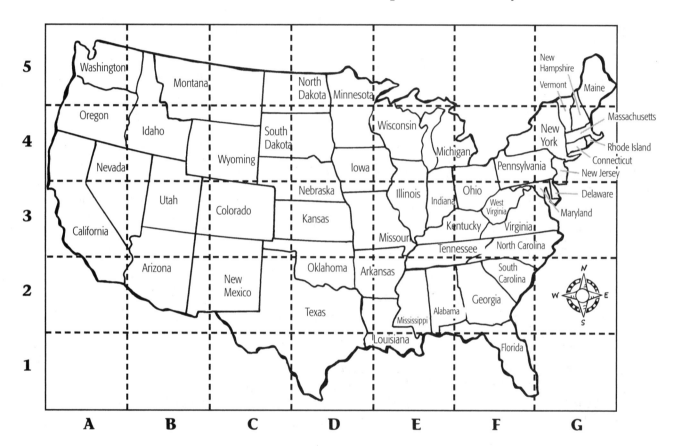

Use the information in the map to answer the questions.

1 Which state is located entirely in F2? _____

2 Which state is located entirely in F3? _____

3 Which state is located mostly in C3? _____

4 Which state is further west, Arizona or New Mexico? _____

5 Which state is further north, Maine or Florida? _____

47

First Presidents

Keeping track of the U. S. presidents can be tricky. Completing this chart will help. First, study the dates in the Term column. Then put the presidents in order by writing the numbers 1 through 10 in the Order column to the left of each name.

Order	Presidents	Term	Vice Presidents
_____	John Adams	1797–1801	Thomas Jefferson
_____	John Quincy Adams	1825–1829	John C. Calhoun
_____	William Henry Harrison	1841	John Tyler
_____	Andrew Jackson	1829–1837	John C. Calhoun, Martin Van Buren
_____	George Washington	1789–1797	John Adams
_____	Thomas Jefferson	1801–1809	Aaron Burr, George Clinton
_____	James Madison	1809–1817	George Clinton, Elbridge Gerry
_____	James Monroe	1817–1835	Daniel D. Tompkins
_____	John Tyler	1841–1845	no vice president
_____	Martin Van Buren	1837–1841	Richard M. Johnson

Use the chart to answer the questions.

1 Who was president when Elbridge Gerry was vice president?

_____

2 Which men were both presidents and vice presidents?

_____

3 Which vice presidents served two different presidents?

_____

4 Who was president for the shortest amount of time?

_____

5 Who was vice president in both 1809 and 1810?

_____

Name _____ Date _____

Math on the Menu

Are you hungry? Study the restaurant menu below.

Denise's Dandy Diner

APPETIZERS
Tomato Soup 3.25
Chips and Salsa 2.25
Stuffed Mushrooms 4.50

_____ 5.00

DRINKS
Iced Tea 1.75
Milk 1.50

_____ 2.00

MAIN COURSE
Meatloaf 6.95
Spaghetti
and Meat Balls 5.75
Pork Chops
and Applesauce 6.25
Roasted Chicken 6.50
Pasta Primavera 5.25

_____ 6.85

SIDE ITEMS
Salad 3.50
Red Beans and Rice 3.00
Cole Slaw 2.50

_____ 3.25

DESSERTS
Brownie 3.75
Peach Pie 4.25

_____ 3.60

Use the information in the menu to answer the questions.

1 How much does the meatloaf cost? _____

2 What item costs $3.75? _____

3 How much more does the roasted chicken cost than the pork chops?

_____

4 How much do spaghetti and a salad cost all together? _____

5 Add the names of the foods below to the menu. Remember to write each

one in the correct category.

Cupcake   Juice   Sweet Potatoes   Clam Dip   Baked Fish

Name _____   Date _____

Cookie Competition

Start your ovens: It's the great cookie bake off! Our finalists are competing to be crowned cookie champ. They have five hours to see how many cookies they can bake. Who won? To find out, study the graphs below.

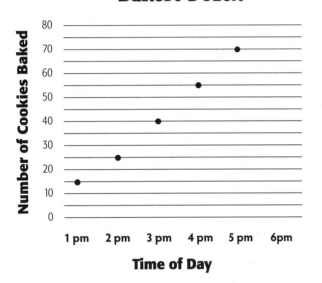

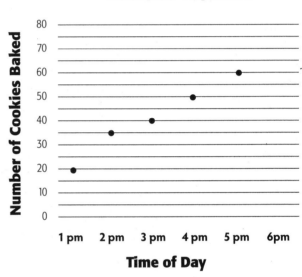

Use information from the line graphs to answer the questions.

1 By 6 pm, Baker's Dozen baked another 10 cookies. How many did they bake all together? Mark your answer on the graph and draw a line to connect all of the points.

2 By 6 pm, Cookie's Cutters baked another 15 cookies. How many did they bake all together? Mark your answer on the graph and draw a line to connect all of the points.

3 How many cookies had Cookie's Cutters baked at 2 pm? _____

4 What happened in the contest at 3 pm? _____

5 Who won the contest? By how many cookies? _____

Name _____ Date _____

Double Feature

Tara loves going to the movies and eating popcorn. But ticket prices have gone up. Even popcorn costs more! To learn how much more, study the double bar graph below.

Going to the Movies

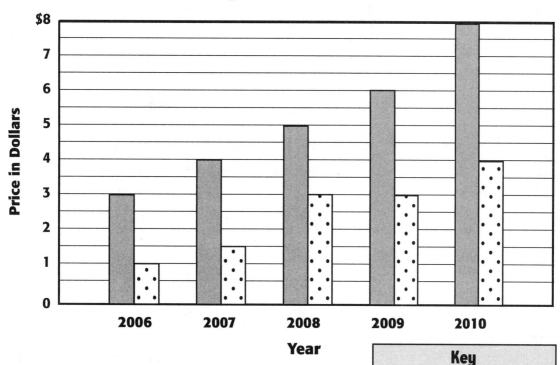

Use the information in the graph to answer the questions.

Key

Ticket = ▓

Popcorn = ⫶⫶

1 How much was one movie ticket in 2008? _____

2 How much was popcorn in 2007? _____

3 How much more was popcorn in 2007 than in 2006? _____

4 How much was a ticket and a popcorn in 2009? _____

5 Between what two years did the price of popcorn increase the most? _____

Name _____ Date _____

Bunny Babies

Bob loves his bunnies, but keeping track of all his pets is a chore at Big Bob's Bunny Farm. Study and complete the pictograph to find out how many bunnies Bob has on his farm each month. Remember to look at the Key.

Key	
🐰 =	10 bunnies
🥕 =	5 bunnies

January 🐰 = _____ bunnies

April 🐰 🐰 🥕 = _____ bunnies

July 🐰 🐰 🐰 🥕 = _____ bunnies

October 🐰 🐰 🐰 🐰 🐰 = _____ bunnies

Record your answers on the line graph. Draw a dot over each month showing the number of bunnies on the farm. Then draw a line to connect the dots.

Big Bob's Bunny Farm

Number of Bunnies: 50, 45, 40, 35, 30, 25, 20, 15, 10, 5, 0

Month: January April July October

1 In which month did Bob have the fewest bunnies? _____

2 How many more bunnies did Bob have in July than in April? _____

3 How many more bunnies did Bob have in October than

in January? _____

Time to Travel

Zone Map

What time is it? Well, that depends. Where are you right now?
Study the map to learn about standard time zones.

Use the information in the map to answer the questions.

1　It is 4 pm in Alabama. What time is it in Minnesota? _____

2　You are in Colorado. It is 4 pm. If you call a friend in Virginia, what time
is it there? _____

3　You fly from Oregon to Missouri. When you arrive in Missouri, it's 5 pm
there. What time is it in Oregon? _____

4　It is 10:30 am in New Mexico. What time is it in Kansas? _____

5　What time zone are you in? _____

Name _____ Date _____

Airport Antics

Traveling is fun, but it is important to know when to arrive at the airport and where to go once you get there. Study the table below to help you find your way.

GOING TO	LEAVING AT	STATUS	GATE
Boston	4:15pm	departed	72
Atlanta	5:10pm	delayed	24
New York	6:05pm	boarding	15
Chicago	6:55pm	on time	61
Seattle	7:20pm	on time	19
Los Angeles	7:45pm	cancelled	44
Philadelphia	8:30pm	delayed	31
Tucson	8:40pm	on time	17
St. Louis	8:45pm	on time	21
New Orleans	9:00pm	delayed	25

Use the information in the table to answer the questions.

1 You are flying to Tucson. What gate do you go to? _____

2 Which flights are delayed? _____

_____

3 Which flight leaves from gate 19? _____

4 What is the status of the flight leaving from gate 44? _____

5 Which flight leaves later, the one to St. Louis or the one

to Chicago? _____

6 The next flight to leave the airport is boarding now. Where is it going?

_____

Name _____ Date _____

Compass Directions

Are you lost? To find your way through town, follow the directions below.

N

	Grocery Grove			Central Elementary
First Bank of Bucks		Downtown Bikes		
			Betty's Diner	
	POST OFFICE			
	Angie's Auto Parts			Wig Shop

W   **E**

Start ➡

S

Read the directions and draw a line to show your route.

1 Go east for two blocks.

2 Go north for three blocks.

3 Go west for one block.

4 Go south for two blocks.

5 Go east for three blocks.

6 Go north for three blocks.

7 Go west for one block.

8 Go south for three blocks.

9 What business are you the closest to? _____

Name _____ Date _____

Graphing Fun and Games | Double Bar Graph

The store Too Terrific Toys is selling two terrific toys! Their rocket ships and chemistry sets are very popular. Which toy sold the most? Study the double bar graph below.

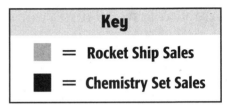

Key

▨ = **Rocket Ship Sales**

■ = **Chemistry Set Sales**

Spring Toy Sales

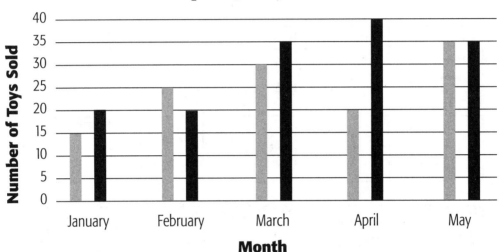

Use the information in the double bar graph to answer the questions.

1 How many rocket ships sold in January? _____

2 In which months did the store sell more chemistry sets than rocket ships? _____

3 In which month did the store sell the same number of rocket ships and chemistry sets? _____

4 Which toy sold most in April? _____

How much more? _____

5 How many chemistry sets were sold all together? _____

Answer Key

PAGE 7
1. 17 feet
2. 6 feet
3. 12 feet
4. 1 foot
5. Answers will vary.

PAGE 8
Order: 1, 7, 2, 5, 3, 6, 4, 8
1. Saturn
2. Neptune
3. Mars
4. Jupiter

PAGE 9
1. golf
2. Answers will vary, depending on the current date.
3. Joey Sticks
4. Marvelous Mud Pies
5. 2 years, 1 day

PAGE 10
1. flashlight
2. sleeping bag
3. 19
4. 35
5. flip flops and address book

PAGE 11
1. pumpkin pie, 24
2. plum pudding, 7
3. 10
4. 71
5. Answers will vary.

PAGE 12
1. 14
2. 12
3. 4
4. 7
5. 40

PAGE 13
1. basketball practice
2. Wednesday, 5:30
3. eating pizza
4. Monday and Wednesday
5. 4:30

PAGE 14
1. 6
2. raisins, 8
3. 9
4. apples and cheese sticks
5. 22

PAGE 15
1. 3
2. 2
3. 3
4. 2
5. 16

PAGE 16
1. 4
2. 1
3. 3
4. 1
5. boys who like dogs, 2

PAGE 17

1. 26
2. 2
3. 21
4. 6
5. 15

PAGE 18

1. $75
2. refreshments, $35
3. $7
4. $294
5. $384

PAGE 19

Presidents:
Theodore Roosevelt
Abraham Lincoln
George Washington

Places:
desert
Yellowstone Park
city
beach

Animals:
gorilla
bird
dolphin
fox

Holidays:
Independence Day
Halloween
Valentine's Day
Thanksgiving

PAGE 20

1. 5 chips
2. 180
3. Tasty Tortilla Treats
4. Nutty Nuts Peanut Butter,
   5 milligrams
5. 4 grams

PAGE 21

1. soccer
2. soccer
3. 10
4. 7
5. 68

PAGE 22

1. 6
2. Sandy Bend Sweepers, away
3. Friday, May 13
4. 2
5. 7

PAGE 23

Students should fill in chart to
show these balances:
$5
$11
$10
$14
$12
$17
$20
$16
$21
$21

PAGE 24
1. 3
2. 1
3. 2
4. 4
5. 30

PAGE 25
1. 70
2. 65
3. 215
4. 2,150
5. 50

PAGE 26
1. 11
2. 4
3. 5
4. the number that I. M. and R. U. ate together, 2
5. 37

PAGE 27
1. 70
2. 80
3. 90
4. 340
5. 60

PAGE 28
1. 4
2. 12
3. 2
4. 4
5. 48

PAGE 29
1. 600
2. 500
3. 800
4. 200
5. 3,600

PAGE 30
Rank: 6, 8, 2, 9, 7, 1, 4, 10, 3, 5
1. Gary Gamer
2. Eyes on the Prize
3. Digitz
4. 375
5. The Count, Vid Kid, Number Gal

PAGE 31
1. July
2. topaz
3. June
4. daisy
5. ruby

PAGE 32
1. lion
2. Sagittarius
3. Libra
4. April 20–May 20

PAGE 33
1. 15
2. 60
3. 60
4. 2006, 2008, 2010
5. 205

PAGE 34
1. $325
2. $425
3. $225
4. $800
5. $1,000

PAGE 35
1. 25
2. 10
3. 2007, 2008, 2010
4. 2005
5. 2008

PAGE 36
1. 13 hours
2. 18 hours, less, 2 hours
3. giraffe
4. A bar reflecting 6 hours should be marked on the graph.
5. Answers will vary, and a bar reflecting the answer should be marked on the graph.

PAGE 37
1. Topeka
2. flowering dogwood
3. New York
4. Hawaii, 1959
5. Olympia
6. Kansas

PAGE 38
1. 18
2. 29
3. 7
4. 9
5. 115

PAGE 39
1. 0
2. 45
3. 34
4. 3
5. 184

PAGE 40
1. 15
2. 15
3. 3rd grade and 5th grade
4. A bar reflecting 55 eggs should be marked on the graph.

PAGE 41
1. 9
2. 8
3. 36
4. 4, 6, 12
5. yellow and blue

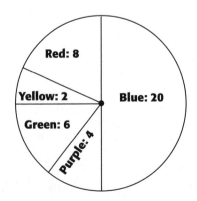

PAGE 42
1. 35
2. 2
3. $6.25
4. $1.50
5. $11.25

PAGE 43
1. $1.50
2. $3.00
3. $0.25
4. eggs
5. $1.00

PAGE 44
1. 4 cents/minute
2. 2 cents/minute
3. 2 cents/minute
4. Call Again
5. $0.30
6. Call Again

PAGE 45
1. 45 miles per hour
2. 200 miles per hour
3. 25 miles per hour
4. 155 miles per hour
5. giraffe and dog

PAGE 46

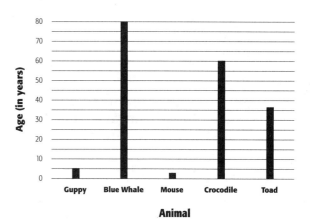

1. blue whale
2. 2 years
3. 44 years
4. 57 years

PAGE 47
1. Georgia
2. West Virginia
3. Colorado
4. Arizona
5. Maine

PAGE 48
Order: 2, 6, 9, 7, 1, 3, 4, 5, 10, 8
1. James Madison
2. John Adams, Thomas Jefferson, Martin Van Buren, and John Tyler
3. John C. Calhoun and George Clinton
4. William Henry Harrison
5. George Clinton

PAGE 49

1. $6.95

2. brownie

3. $0.25

4. $9.25

5. Appetizer: Clam Dip, Drink: Juice, Main Course: Baked Fish, Side Item: Sweet Potatoes, Dessert: Cupcake

PAGE 50

1. 80

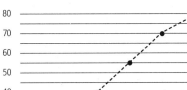

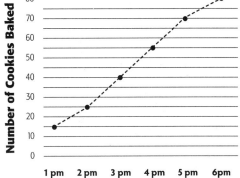

2. 75

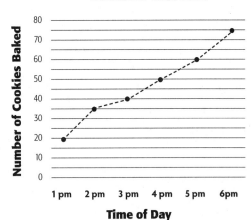

3. 35

4. both groups had baked the same number of cookies

5. Baker's Dozen, 5 cookies

PAGE 51

1. $5.00

2. $1.50

3. $0.50

4. $9.00

5. 2007 and 2008

PAGE 52

Pictograph data: 10, 25, 35, 50

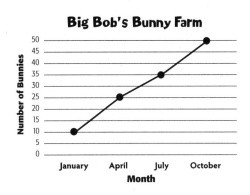

1. January

2. 10

3. 40

PAGE 53

1. 4:00 P.M.

2. 6:00 P.M.

3. 3:00 P.M.

4. 11:30 A.M.

5. Answers will vary, but should reflect the local time zone.

PAGE 54

1. 17

2. Atlanta, Philadelphia, and New Orleans

3. Seattle

4. cancelled

5. St. Louis

6. New York

PAGE 55

Betty's Diner

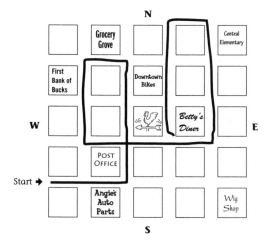

PAGE 56

1. 15

2. January, March, and April

3. May

4. chemistry sets, 20

5. 150

Notes